CHOCOLATE BRANDY CAKES

Chocolate Brandy Cakes

Jialin Tian, Ph.D.

Text and photographs copyright © 2021 by Jialin Tian

All rights reserved. No part of this book may be reproduced or transmitted in any form or by any means, electronic or mechanical, including photocopying, recording, or by any information storage and retrieval system, without permission in writing from the publisher.

Disclaimer: While every precaution has been taken in the preparation of this book, the publisher and author assume no responsibility for errors or omissions, or for damage or loss resulting directly or indirectly from the use of the information contained herein.

Published in the United States by Jayca

ISBN 978-1-7334779-2-5

First Edition 2021
www.macaronmagic.com

To my mother, Yabin

CONTENTS

INTRODUCTION 6

CHERRY BRANDY (KIRSCHWASSER) 8
Cherry #1: White Chocolate Cherry Cake 10
Cherry #2: Dark Chocolate Walnut Cake 12
Cherry #3: Milk Chocolate Puff Pastry Crown 14
Cherry #4: Milk Chocolate Cherry Crown 16
Cherry #5: Chocolate Walnut Bundt Cake 18

Cherry #6: White Chocolate Round Cake 20
Cherry #7: White Chocolate Almond Cake 22
Cherry #8: Dark Chocolate Cherry Cupcakes 24
Cherry #9: White Chocolate Raspberry Cake Ring 26
Cherry #10: Raspberry and Cherry Hazelnut Crown 28
Cherry #11: Dark Chocolate Raspberry Loaves 30
Cherry #12: Raspberry Walnut Cupcakes 32
Cherry #13: Milk Chocolate Raspberry Loaves 34

APPLE BRANDY (CALVADOS)   36
Apple #1: Milk Chocolate Apple Crown   38
Apple #2: Dark Chocolate Puff Pastry Crown   40
Apple #3: Cream Cheese Apple Cake   42
Apple #4: Dark Chocolate Apple and Macadamia Cakes   44
Apple #5: Apple Upside-Down Cake   46
Apple #6: Apple Bundt Cake   48
Apple #7: Dark Chocolate Apple and Walnut Cake   50

Apple #8: Dark Chocolate Macadamia Apple Cake   52
Apple #9: Chocolate Pear Round Cake   54
Apple #10: Dark Chocolate Pear Cakes   56
Apple #11: Milk Chocolate Hazelnut Pear Cake   58
Apple #12: Apple Marble Cakes   60
Apple #13: Apple Coffee Cake   62

INTRODUCTION

In this second installment of the baking with spirits collection, we focus on fruit brandies. In particular, we explore the possibilities of baking with the intriguing duo of kirsch and calvados. The word "brandy" is derived from the Dutch word *brandewijn*, meaning "burnt wine." As the name suggests, a brandy is a distilled spirit. Both kirsch and calvados possess the distinctive aroma of distilled spirits, with a layer of fruity notes. Baking with brandy can be challenging because when the alcohol evaporates, so does some of the brandy's essence and aroma.

To preserve brandy's delicate flavor in baked goods, we use a list of ingredients similar to the one we used when baking with whiskey. These ingredients complement the spirit. Almond flour, low in starch, high in protein, has a subtle sweet aroma and is an ideal mate for fruit brandies. Cream cheese also works wonders with brandies. The enzymes in cream cheese interact with the alcohol, which can improve the taste and add complexity to baked goods. Chocolate is another main ingredient. The bittersweet aroma of dark chocolate and cocoa add richness to cakes. The sweetness of milk chocolate and white chocolate counterbalances the power of the brandy. In addition, we incorporate brandy-infused fresh fruit into the recipes; by doing so, we enhance the flavors of the brandies in the finished products without overpowering the other flavors.

Kirschwasser (German for "cherry water") originated in the Black Forest of southern Germany. Traditionally, it is produced by the double distillation of fermented cherry juice. The black morello variety is commonly chosen. Kirsch is made in the *eau-de-vie* style which is clear, dry, and unaged. It has a signature aroma of bitter almonds or marzipan. Kirsch is no stranger to baking. Fans of the ever-popular Black Forest cake (*Schwarzwälder Kirschtorte*) are familiar with the taste of kirsch in pastry—dark chocolate sponge cakes are moistened with kirsch and layered with fresh cherries and whipped cream. To highlight the kirsch but without making the cake too "alcoholic," most recipes in this book use kirsch-infused cherries to heighten the aroma and taste. The resulting cakes are moist, tender, and full of marzipan flavor but without the bitterness of raw alcohol. Nuts and chocolates add extra richness and texture. The leftover infusion kirsch can be enjoyed as an aperitif or dessert liqueur. It is sweetened by fresh cherry juice which also dilutes the alcohol.

Calvados, a close cousin of cognac, is distilled from fermented apple juice (some versions add pears). Produced in France's Lower Normandy, calvados is the signature spirit of the region. Normandy's cool climate isn't suited to the cultivation of grapes; instead, the region is home to abundant apple and pear orchards. The apples in calvados production can be sweet, bitter, bittersweet, or acidic. Unlike kirsch, calvados is aged in large oak barrels that give calvados its golden-caramel hue. The flavor profile of calvados is comparable to that of cognac, but with a hint of fresh apple. We use fresh apples and pears as the media for calvados. With calvados-infused apples and pears, walnuts, and chocolates, these cakes are the perfect comfort dessert in fall or winter. The leftover liquid from the infusion can be enjoyed as a dessert wine.

I hope you will enjoy baking these twenty-six splendid creations with kirsch and calvados! Most of all, I hope that you will proudly share the fruit of your labor with family and friends.

Cheers!

CHERRY BRANDY

KIRSCHWASSER

CHOCOLATE BRANDY CAKES

INGREDIENTS *(Yield: one 20-cm/8-in loaf cake)*

Brandied Cherries:

150 g/5.3 oz red cherries, pitted

Kirsch

Cake Batter:

100 g/3.5 oz almond flour

200 g/7.1 oz all-purpose flour

50 g/1.8 oz light brown sugar

7.5 g/0.26 oz (1½ tsp) baking powder

1.25 g/0.044 oz (¼ tsp) baking soda

Pinch of salt

50 g/1.8 oz unsalted butter, at room temperature

100 g/3.5 oz sour cream

20 g/0.71 oz kirsch

5 eggs

100 g/3.5 oz white chocolate chips

Glaze:

100 g/3.5 oz white chocolate chips

100 g/3.5 oz sour cream

20 g/0.71 oz kirsch

Cherry #1
White Chocolate Cherry Cake

In a container, cover the pitted cherries with kirsch. Allow the cherries to soak for a few hours or overnight.

For the cake batter, in a mixer bowl, combine the almond flour, flour, sugar, baking powder, baking soda, and salt. Attach the bowl to a stand mixer fitted with a paddle attachment. Mix well. Blend in the butter, sour cream, kirsch, and eggs. Mix again to combine. Finally, fold the white chocolate chips into the batter.

Remove the macerated cherries from the soaking liquid using a strainer. Dice the cherries into small pieces and reserve.

Generously butter a 20-cm/8-in loaf pan. Pour about half of the batter into the pan. Add an even layer of the diced cherries, and then add the remaining batter. Bake the cake at 185°C/365°F for about 40 minutes. Let the cake cool slightly before unmolding.

For the glaze, melt the white chocolate chips in a microwave oven; stir the chocolate chips every 30 seconds to avoid burning. Stir the sour cream and kirsch into melted chocolate. Glaze the cake with the white chocolate icing. Allow the icing to set before serving.

INGREDIENTS *(Yield: one 20-cm/8-in loaf cake)*

Brandied Cherries:

150 g/5.3 oz red cherries, pitted

Kirsch

Cake Batter:

100 g/3.5 oz almond flour

200 g/7.1 oz all-purpose flour

50 g/1.8 oz cocoa powder

100 g/3.5 oz light brown sugar

10 g/0.35 oz (2 tsp) baking powder

Pinch of salt

100 g/3.5 oz unsalted butter, at room temperature

4 eggs

20 g/0.71 oz kirsch

100 g/3.5 oz whole milk

100 g/3.5 oz walnut pieces

Glaze:

100 g/3.5 oz heavy cream

75 g/2.6 oz milk chocolate chips

20 g/0.71 oz kirsch

50 g/1.8 oz walnut pieces

Cherry #2
Dark Chocolate Walnut Cake

In a container, cover the pitted cherries with kirsch. Allow the cherries to soak for a few hours or overnight.

Remove the macerated cherries from the soaking liquid using a strainer. Dice the cherries into small pieces and reserve.

For the cake batter, in a mixer bowl, combine the almond flour, flour, cocoa powder, sugar, baking powder, and salt. Attach the bowl to a stand mixer fitted with a paddle attachment. Mix well. Blend in the softened butter, eggs, kirsch, and milk. Mix again to combine. Finally, fold the walnut pieces and diced cherries into the batter.

Generously butter a 20-cm/8-in loaf pan. Pour the batter into the pan. Bake the cake at 185°C/365°F for about 35 minutes. Cool slightly and unmold the cake.

For the glaze, boil the cream in a saucepan. Pour the hot cream over the milk chocolate chips in a mixing bowl. Stir the mixture until smooth. Add the kirsch and walnut pieces into the mixture. Glaze the cake with the icing. Allow the icing to set slightly before serving.

INGREDIENTS *(Yield: one 20-cm/8-in cake)*

Puff Pastry Cake:

400 g/14.1 oz puff pastry dough

30 g/1.1 oz unsalted butter, at room temperature

40 g/1.4 oz granulated sugar

200 g/7.1 oz milk chocolate chips

20 g/0.71 oz kirsch

20 g/0.71 oz raw sugar crystals (optional)

Glaze:

50 g/1.8 oz cherry puree

50 g/1.8 oz milk chocolate chips

15 g/0.53 oz kirsch

Cherry #3
Milk Chocolate Puff Pastry Crown

Cut the puff pastry dough into 3.8-cm/1.5-in pieces and reserve. Butter a 20-cm/8-in tube pan. Layer the dough pieces to cover the bottom of the pan and about 1.3-cm/0.5-in up the side. Reserve the remaining dough pieces. Sprinkle about half of the sugar on top.

Melt the chocolate chips in a microwave oven; stir the chocolate chips every 30 seconds to avoid burning. Stir the kirsch into melted chocolate. Spread the mixture on top of the puff pastry dough. Add a second layer of the puff pastry dough pieces. Cover the top with the remaining granulated sugar and raw sugar crystals (optional). Bake the cake at 185°C/365°F for about 40 minutes.

For the glaze, boil the cherry puree in a saucepan. Pour the hot puree over the milk chocolate chips in a mixing bowl. Stir the mixture until smooth. Add the kirsch and stir again. Glaze the cake with the icing. Allow the glaze to set before serving.

INGREDIENTS *(Yield: one 20-cm/8-in cake)*

Brandied Cherries:

450 g/1 lb red cherries, pitted

Kirsch

Cake Batter:

100 g/3.5 oz almond flour

200 g/7.1 oz all-purpose flour

50 g/1.8 oz light brown sugar

10 g/0.35 oz (1 Tbsp) instant dry yeast

Pinch of salt

150 g/5.3 oz unsalted butter, at room temperature

200 g/7.1 oz almond paste

4 eggs

100 g/3.5 oz whole milk

30 g/1.1 oz kirsch

150 g/5.3 oz milk chocolate chips

150 g/5.3 oz walnut pieces

Coating for the Pan:

50 g/1.8 oz unsalted butter, at room temperature

50 g/1.8 oz light brown sugar

Cherry #4
Milk Chocolate Cherry Crown

In a container, cover the pitted cherries with kirsch. Allow the cherries to soak for a few hours or overnight.

For the cake batter, in a mixer bowl, combine the almond flour, flour, sugar, yeast, and salt. Attach the bowl to a stand mixer fitted with a paddle attachment. Mix well. Blend in the butter and almond paste. Add the eggs, milk, and kirsch. Mix again to combine. Finally, fold the chocolate chips and walnut pieces into the batter. Cover the bowl with plastic wrap. Allow the batter to rise at room temperature overnight.

On the following day, remove the macerated cherries from the soaking liquid using a strainer and reserve.

Butter a 20-cm/8-in tube pan. Evenly coat the bottom of the pan with light brown sugar. Arrange the kirsch-infused cherries at the bottom of the pan. Pour the cake batter into the pan. Cover the pan with plastic wrap and allow the cake to rest at room temperature for an hour.

Bake the cake at 185°C/365°F for about 40 minutes. Invert the cake onto a plate when it is still warm.

INGREDIENTS *(Yield: one 23-cm/9-in cake)*

Cake Batter:

100 g/3.5 oz almond flour

200 g/7.1 oz all-purpose flour

100 g/3.5 oz light brown sugar

10 g/0.35 oz (2 tsp) baking powder

50 g/1.8 oz cocoa powder

Pinch of salt

100 g/3.5 oz sour cream

3 eggs

100 g/3.5 oz whole milk

30 g/1.1 oz kirsch

200 g/7.1 oz white chocolate chips

Glaze:

100 g/3.5 oz white chocolate chips

100 g/3.5 oz sour cream

20 g/0.71 oz kirsch

50 g/1.8 oz walnut pieces

Chocolate Covered Cherries:

100 g/3.5 oz white chocolate chips

85 g/3 oz heavy cream

15 g/0.53 oz kirsch

30 red cherries

Cherry #5 Chocolate Walnut Bundt Cake

For the cake batter, in a mixer bowl, combine the almond flour, flour, sugar, baking powder, cocoa powder, and salt. Attach the bowl to a stand mixer fitted with a paddle attachment. Mix well. Blend in the sour cream, eggs, milk, and kirsch. Mix again to combine. Finally, stir the white chocolate chips into the batter.

Generously butter a 23-cm/9-in Bundt pan. Pour the batter into the Bundt pan. Bake the cake at 185°C/365°F for about 45 minutes. Let cool slightly before unmolding the cake.

For the glaze, melt the chocolate chips in a microwave oven; stir the chocolate chips every 30 seconds to avoid burning. Mix the sour cream with melted chocolate. Add the kirsch and walnut pieces. Mix well. Pour the icing on top of the cake.

To make chocolate covered cherries, melt the chocolate chips in a microwave oven. Stir the cream and kirsch into melted chocolate. Wait until the ganache is thickened. Dip the cherries into the ganache. Let the cherries set on a plate for a few hours. Garnish the cake with chocolate covered cherries if desired.

INGREDIENTS *(Yield: one 23-cm/9-in round cake)*

Brandied Cherries:

20 red cherries, pitted

Kirsch

Cake Batter:

100 g/3.5 oz almond flour

100 g/3.5 oz all-purpose flour

50 g/1.8 oz light brown sugar

5 g/0.18 oz (1 tsp) baking powder

1.25 g/0.044 oz (¼ tsp) baking soda

Pinch of salt

100 g/3.5 oz cream cheese, at room temperature

50 g/1.8 oz unsalted butter, at room temperature

6 eggs

30 g/1.1 oz kirsch

100 g/3.5 oz milk chocolate chips

Cherry #6
White Chocolate Round Cake

In a container, cover the pitted cherries with kirsch. Allow the cherries to soak for a few hours or overnight.

For the cake batter, in a mixer bowl, combine the almond flour, flour, sugar, baking powder, baking soda, and salt. Attach the bowl to a stand mixer fitted with a paddle attachment. Mix well. Blend in the cream cheese and butter, and then add the eggs and kirsch. Mix again to combine. Finally, fold the chocolate chips into the batter.

Remove the macerated cherries from the soaking liquid using a strainer and reserve.

Generously butter a 23-cm/9-in round cake pan. Pour the batter into the pan. Add the reserved cherries into the batter. Bake the cake at 185°C/365°F for about 35 minutes. Invert the cake onto a plate when it is still warm.

INGREDIENTS *(Yield: one 20-cm/8-in loaf cake)*

Brandied Cherries:

10 red cherries, pitted

Kirsch

Cake Batter:

100 g/3.5 oz almond flour

200 g/7.1 oz all-purpose flour

30 g/1.1 oz light brown sugar

10 g/0.35 oz (1 Tbsp) instant dry yeast

Pinch of salt

100 g/3.5 oz butter, at room temperature

50 g/1.8 oz cream cheese, at room temperature

4 eggs

30 g/1.1 oz kirsch

100 g/3.5 oz white chocolate chips

Topping:

50 g/1.8 oz almond paste

50 g/1.8 oz sliced almonds

1 egg

20 g/0.71 oz heavy cream

15 g/0.53 oz kirsch

Cherry #7
White Chocolate Almond Cake

In a container, cover the pitted cherries with kirsch. Allow the cherries to soak for a few hours or overnight.

For the batter, in a mixer bowl, combine the almond flour, flour, sugar, yeast, and salt. Attach the bowl to a stand mixer fitted with a paddle attachment. Mix well. Blend in the butter and cream cheese. Add the eggs and kirsch. Mix again to combine. Finally, fold the chocolate chips into the batter. Cover the bowl with plastic wrap. Allow the batter to rise at room temperature overnight.

On the following day, remove the macerated cherries from the soaking liquid using a strainer and reserve.

Generously butter a 20-cm/8-in loaf pan. Pour about half of the batter into the pan; add the reserved cherries. Pour the remaining batter on top of the cherries. Cover and allow the batter to rest at room temperature for about 40 minutes.

Meanwhile, combine all the ingredients for the topping in a bowl. Mix well. Spread the topping mixture over the batter. Bake the loaf at 185°C/365°F for about 30 minutes. Let cool slightly before unmolding the cake.

INGREDIENTS *(Yield: 12 cupcakes)*

Brandied Cherries:

150 g/5.3 oz red cherries, pitted

Kirsch

Cake Batter:

75 g/2.6 oz almond flour

75 g/2.6 oz all-purpose flour

25 g/0.88 oz cocoa powder

50 g/1.8 oz light brown sugar

7.5 g/0.26 oz (1½ tsp) baking powder

1.25 g/0.044 oz (¼ tsp) baking soda

Pinch of salt

75 g/2.6 oz sour cream

75 g/2.6 oz unsalted butter, at room temperature

15 g/0.53 oz kirsch

3 eggs

Frosting:

230 g/8.1 oz cream cheese, at room temperature

75 g/2.6 oz unsalted butter, at room temperature

50 g/1.8 oz light brown sugar

75 g/2.6 oz milk chocolate chips

25 g/0.88 oz kirsch

Chocolate Covered Cherries:

100 g/3.5 oz milk chocolate chips

85 g/3 oz heavy cream

15 g/0.53 oz kirsch

30 red cherries

Raw sugar crystals

Cherry #8
Dark Chocolate Cherry Cupcakes

In a container, cover the pitted cherries with kirsch. Allow the cherries to soak for a few hours or overnight. Remove the macerated cherries from the soaking liquid using a strainer. Dice the cherries into small pieces and reserve.

For the cake batter, in a mixer bowl, combine the almond flour, flour, cocoa powder, sugar, baking powder, baking soda, and salt. Attach the bowl to a stand mixer fitted with a paddle attachment. Mix well. Blend in the sour cream and butter. Add the diced cherries, kirsch, and eggs. Mix again to combine.

Line a regular 12-muffin pan with paper baking cups. Pour the batter into each cup to about 80% full. Bake the cakes at 185°C/365°F for about 25 minutes. Let the cupcakes cool completely.

For the frosting, using a stand mixer fitted with a whisk attachment to whisk the cream cheese, butter, and sugar until fluffy. Melt the milk chocolate chips in a microwave oven; stir every 30 seconds to avoid burning. Let cool slightly. Add the melted milk chocolate chips and kirsch into the frosting. Whisk again until the mixture is light and smooth. Fill a large pastry bag fitted with a star tip with the frosting; pipe the cream on top of the cakes.

To make chocolate covered cherries, melt the chocolate chips in a microwave oven; stir the chocolate chips every 30 seconds to avoid burning. Stir in the cream and kirsch. Wait until the ganache is thickened. Dip the cherries into the ganache. Let the cherries set on a plate for a few hours. Roll the cherries in raw sugar crystals if desired. Decorate the cupcakes with chocolate covered cherries.

INGREDIENTS *(Yield: one 20-cm/8-in cake)*

Brandied Raspberries:

150 g/5.3 oz raspberries

Kirsch

Cake Batter:

100 g/3.5 oz almond flour

200 g/7.1 oz all-purpose flour

50 g/1.8 oz granulated sugar

10 g/0.35 oz (2 tsp) baking powder

Pinch of salt

150 g/5.3 oz unsalted butter, at room temperature

4 eggs

100 g/3.5 oz whole milk

150 g/5.3 oz white chocolate chips

Topping:

200 g/7.1 oz cream cheese, at room temperature

200 g/7.1 oz almond paste

30 g/1.1 oz kirsch

50 g/1.8 oz sliced almonds

Cherry #9
White Chocolate Raspberry Cake Ring

In a container, cover the raspberries with kirsch. Allow the raspberries to soak for a few hours or overnight.

For the cake batter, in a mixer bowl, combine the almond flour, flour, sugar, baking powder, and salt. Attach the bowl to a stand mixer fitted with a paddle attachment. Mix well. Blend in the butter, eggs, and milk. Mix again to combine. Finally, fold the chocolate chips into the batter.

Remove the macerated raspberries from the soaking liquid using a strainer and reserve.

Generously butter a 20-cm/8-in tube pan. Pour the batter into the pan. Place the reserved raspberries on top of the batter.

Mix all the ingredients for the topping in a bowl. Spread the topping mixture on top of the batter. Bake the cake at 185°C/365°F for about 45 minutes. Let cool slightly before unmolding the cake.

INGREDIENTS *(Yield: one 20-cm/8-in cake)*

Cake Batter:

100 g/3.5 oz almond flour

100 g/3.5 oz hazelnut flour

200 g/7.1 oz all-purpose flour

100 g/3.5 oz light brown sugar

50 g/1.8 oz cocoa powder

15 g/0.53 oz (1 Tbsp) baking powder

2.5 oz/0.088 oz (½ tsp) baking soda

Pinch of salt

100 g/3.5 oz unsalted butter, at room temperature

100 g/3.5 oz sour cream

6 eggs

30 g/1.1 oz kirsch

100 g/3.5 oz raspberry puree

200 g/7.1 oz walnut pieces

Frosting:

100 g/3.5 oz dark chocolate chips

200 g/7.1 oz cream cheese, at room temperature

20 g/0.71 oz kirsch

Raw sugar crystals

Cherry #10
Raspberry and Cherry Hazelnut Crown

For the cake batter, in a mixer bowl, combine the almond flour, hazelnut flour, flour, sugar, cocoa powder, baking powder, baking soda, and salt. Attach the bowl to a stand mixer fitted with a paddle attachment. Mix well. Blend in the butter and sour cream. Add the eggs, kirsch, and raspberry puree. Mix again to combine. Finally, fold in the walnut pieces.

Butter a 20-cm/8-in tube pan; pour the batter into the pan. Bake the cake at 185°C/365°F for about 35 minutes. Let the cake cool slightly before unmolding.

For the frosting, melt the chocolate chips in a microwave oven; stir the chocolate chips every 30 seconds to avoid burning. Let cool slightly. Whisk the cream cheese and kirsch into the melted chocolate. Cover the cake with the frosting. Sprinkle raw sugar crystals on top if desired.

INGREDIENTS *(Yield: six 10-cm/4-in mini loaves)*

Brandied Raspberries:

100 g/3.5 oz raspberries

Kirsch

Cake Batter:

100 g/3.5 oz hazelnut flour

300 g/10.6 oz all-purpose flour

130 g/4.6 oz light brown sugar

50 g/1.8 oz cocoa powder

10 g/0.35 oz (1 Tbsp) instant dry yeast

Pinch of salt

200 g/7.1 oz cream cheese, at room temperature

6 eggs

30/1.1 oz kirsch

100 g/3.5 oz raspberry puree

200 g/7.1 oz walnut pieces

Topping:

100 g/3.5 oz almond paste

100 g/3.5 oz cream cheese, at room temperature

Raw sugar crystals

Cherry #11
Dark Chocolate Raspberry Loaves

In a container, cover the raspberries with kirsch. Allow the raspberries to soak for a few hours or overnight.

For the cake batter, in a mixer bowl, combine the hazelnut flour, flour, sugar, cocoa powder, yeast, and salt. Attach the bowl to a stand mixer fitted with a paddle attachment. Mix well. Blend in the cream cheese. Add the eggs, kirsch, and raspberry puree. Mix again to combine. Finally, fold the walnut pieces into the batter. Cover the bowl with plastic wrap. Allow the batter to rise at room temperature overnight.

On the following day, remove the macerated raspberries from the soaking liquid using a strainer and reserve.

Pour the batter into six 10-cm/4-in paper loaf pans. Add the kirsch-infused raspberries on top. Cover the loaves with plastic wrap and allow the loaves to rest at room temperature for about 40 minutes.

For the topping, mix the almond paste and cream cheese. Add the mixture on top of the loaves. Sprinkle the top with raw sugar crystals if desired. Bake the cakes at 185°C/365°F for about 20 minutes.

INGREDIENTS *(Yield: 12 cupcakes)*

Brandied Raspberries:

100 g/3.5 oz raspberries

Kirsch

Cake Batter:

100 g/3.5 oz almond flour

100 g/3.5 all-purpose flour

50 g/1.8 oz light brown sugar

5 g/0.18 oz (1 tsp) baking powder

Pinch of salt

50 g/1.8 oz unsalted butter, at room temperature

50 g/1.8 oz cream cheese, at room temperature

3 eggs

15 g/0.53 oz kirsch

100 g/3.5 oz raspberry puree

100 g/3.5 oz milk chocolate chips

100 g/3.5 oz walnut pieces

Topping:

30 g/1.1 oz cream cheese, at room temperature

Raw sugar crystals

Cherry #12
Raspberry Walnut Cupcakes

In a container, cover the raspberries with kirsch. Allow the raspberries to soak for a few hours or overnight.

For the batter, in a mixer bowl, combine the almond flour, flour, sugar, baking powder, and salt. Attach the bowl to a stand mixer fitted with a paddle attachment. Mix well. Blend in the butter and cream cheese. Add the eggs, kirsch, and raspberry puree. Mix again to combine. Finally, fold the chocolate chips and walnut pieces into the batter.

Remove the macerated raspberries from the soaking liquid using a strainer and reserve.

Line a 12-muffin pan with paper baking cups. Add the batter into the cups, and then place the reserved raspberries on top. Add a small amount of the cream cheese and raw sugar crystals on top of each cake. Bake the cakes at 185°C/365°F for 25 minutes.

INGREDIENTS *(Yield: three 10-cm/4-in mini loaves)*

Brandied Raspberries:

150 g/5.3 oz raspberries

Kirsch

Cake Batter:

100 g/3.5 oz hazelnut flour

200 g/7.1 oz all-purpose flour

50 g/1.8 oz light brown sugar

10 g/0.35 oz (2 tsp) baking powder

Pinch of salt

70 g/2.5 oz walnut oil

4 eggs

30 g/1.1 oz kirsch

100 g/3.5 oz raspberry puree

100 g/3.5 oz milk chocolate chips

Topping:

Sliced almonds

Raw sugar crystals

Cherry #13
Milk Chocolate Raspberry Loaves

In a container, cover the raspberries with kirsch. Allow the raspberries to soak for a few hours or overnight. Remove the macerated raspberries from the soaking liquid using a strainer and reserve.

For the cake batter, in a mixer bowl, combine the hazelnut flour, flour, sugar, baking powder, and salt. Attach the bowl to a stand mixer fitted with a paddle attachment. Mix well. Add the walnut oil, eggs, kirsch, and raspberry puree into the mixture. Mix again to combine. Finally, fold the reserved raspberries and chocolate chips into the batter.

Pour the batter into three 10-cm/4-in paper loaf pans. Sprinkle sliced almonds and raw sugar crystals on top of the cakes. Bake the loaves at 185°C/365°F for about 30 minutes.

APPLE BRANDY

CALVADOS

INGREDIENTS *(Yield: one 20-cm/8-in cake)*

Brandied Apples:

2 Granny Smith apples, peeled and cut into small cubes (around 350 g/12.3 oz)

150 g/5.3 oz calvados

75 g/2.6 oz granulated sugar

Cake Batter:

200 g/7.1 oz almond flour

200 g/7.1 oz all-purpose flour

100 g/3.5 oz light brown sugar

10 g/0.35 oz (1 Tbsp) instant dry yeast

Pinch of salt

100 g/3.5 oz unsalted butter, at room temperature

100 g/3.5 oz cream cheese, at room temperature

4 eggs

200 g/7.1 oz whole milk

30 g/1.1 oz calvados

150 g/5.3 oz milk chocolate chips

Coating for the Pan:

50 g/1.8 oz unsalted butter, at room temperature

50 g/1.8 oz light brown sugar

Apple #1
Milk Chocolate Apple Crown

For the brandied apples, combine the apple cubes with calvados and sugar in a covered container. Allow the apple cubes to soak for a few hours or overnight.

For the cake batter, in a mixer bowl, combine the almond flour, flour, sugar, yeast, and salt. Attach the bowl to a stand mixer fitted with a paddle attachment. Mix well. Blend in the softened butter and cream cheese. Add the eggs, milk, and calvados. Mix again to combine. Finally, stir the milk chocolate chips into the batter. Cover the bowl with plastic wrap. Allow the batter to rise at room temperature overnight.

On the following day, butter a 20-cm/8-in tube pan; evenly coat the bottom of the pan with light brown sugar.

Remove the macerated apple cubes from the calvados-sugar mixture using a strainer. Cover the bottom of the baking pan with the apple cubes. Pour the cake batter on top of the apple pieces. Cover the pan with plastic wrap and allow the cake batter to rest at room temperature for about 45 minutes.

Bake the cake at 185°C/365°F for about 40 minutes. Invert the cake onto a plate when it is still warm.

INGREDIENTS *(Yield: one 20-cm/8-in cake)*

Brandied Apples:

4 Granny Smith apples, peeled and cut into small cubes (around 700 g/1.5 lb)

300 g/10.6 oz calvados

150 g/5.3 oz granulated sugar

Cake Batter:

150 g/5.3 oz almond flour

250 g/8.8 oz all-purpose flour

100 g/3.5 oz granulated sugar

50 g/1.8 oz cocoa powder

15 g/0.53 oz (1 Tbsp) baking powder

Pinch of salt

50 g/1.8 oz sour cream

100 g/3.5 oz almond oil

150 g/5.3 oz whole milk

30 g/1.1 oz calvados

4 eggs

150 g/5.3 oz walnut pieces

Topping:

120 g/4.2 oz Puff pastry dough

Granulated sugar

Apple #2
Dark Chocolate Puff Pastry Crown

For the brandied apples, combine the apple cubes with calvados and sugar in a covered container. Allow the apple cubes to soak for a few hours or overnight.

For the cake batter, in a mixer bowl, combine the almond flour, flour, sugar, cocoa powder, baking powder, and salt. Attach the bowl to a stand mixer fitted with a paddle attachment. Mix well. Blend in the sour cream, almond oil, whole milk, calvados, and eggs. Mix again to combine. Fold the walnut pieces into the batter.

Remove the macerated apple cubes from the calvados-sugar mixture using a strainer and reserve.

Generously butter a 20-cm/8-in tube pan. Pour the batter into the tube pan. Scatter the apple cubes on top of the batter. Cut the puff pastry dough into thin pieces, and then cover the apples with the puff pastry pieces. Sprinkle granulated sugar on top. Bake the cake at 191°C/375°F for about 45 minutes. Let cool slightly before unmolding.

INGREDIENTS *(Yield: one 20-cm/8-in loaf cake)*

Brandied Apples:

2 Granny Smith apples, peeled and cut into slices (around 350 g/12.3 oz)

150 g/5.3 oz calvados

75 g/2.6 oz granulated sugar

Cake Batter:

100 g/3.5 oz almond flour

200 g/7.1 oz all-purpose flour

50 g/1.8 oz granulated sugar

10 g/0.35 oz (2 tsp) baking powder

1.25 g/0.044 oz (¼ tsp) baking soda

Pinch of salt

250 g/8.8 oz cream cheese, at room temperature

3 eggs

50 g/1.8 oz whole milk

20 g/0.71 oz calvados

Coating for the Pan:

Unsalted butter, at room temperature

50 g/1.8 oz granulated sugar

Apple #3
Cream Cheese Apple Cake

For the brandied apples, combine the apple slices with calvados and sugar in a covered container. Allow the apple slices to soak for a few hours or overnight.

For the cake batter, in a mixer bowl, combine the almond flour, flour, sugar, baking powder, baking soda, and salt. Attach the bowl to a stand mixer fitted with a paddle attachment. Mix well. Blend in the cream cheese, eggs, milk, and calvados. Mix again to combine.

Remove the macerated apple slices from the calvados-sugar mixture using a strainer and reserve.

Generously butter a 20-cm/8-in loaf pan, and then sprinkle granulated sugar on top. Arrange the reserved apple slices at the bottom of the pan. Pour the batter into the pan. Bake the cake at 191°C/375°F for about an hour. Let cool slightly before unmolding.

INGREDIENTS *(Yield: 4 to 6 large muffin-sized cakes)*

Brandied Apples:

2 Granny Smith apples, peeled and cut into cubes (around 350 g/12.3 oz)

150 g/5.3 oz calvados

75 g/2.6 oz granulated sugar

Cake Batter:

150 g/5.3 oz almond flour

200 g/7.1 oz all-purpose flour

100 g/3.5 oz granulated sugar

30 g/1.1 oz cocoa powder

15 g/0.53 oz (1 Tbsp) baking powder

1.25 g/0.044 oz (¼ tsp) baking soda

Pinch of salt

250 g/8.8 oz cream cheese, at room temperature

4 eggs

30 g/1.1 oz calvados

100 g/3.5 oz milk chocolate chips

Topping:

50 g/1.8 oz Macadamia nuts

Granulated sugar

Apple #4
Dark Chocolate Apple and Macadamia Cakes

For the brandied apples, combine the apple cubes with calvados and sugar in a covered container. Allow the apple cubes to soak for a few hours or overnight.

For the cake batter, in a mixer bowl, combine the almond flour, flour, sugar, cocoa powder, baking powder, baking soda, and salt. Attach the bowl to a stand mixer fitted with a paddle attachment. Mix well. Blend in the cream cheese, eggs, and calvados. Mix again to combine. Fold the chocolate chips into the batter.

Remove the macerated apple cubes from the calvados-sugar mixture using a strainer and reserve.

Pour the batter into large paper baking cups or large muffin pan lined with paper baking cups. Place the reserved apple cubes and macadamia nuts over the batter, and then sprinkle the top with granulated sugar. Bake the cakes at 188°C/370°F for about 25 minutes.

INGREDIENTS *(Yield: one 23-cm/9-in round cake)*

Brandied Apples:

1 Granny Smith apple, peeled and cut into cubes (around 175 g/6.2 oz)

1 Granny Smith apple, peeled and cut into slices (around 175 g/6.2 oz)

150 g/5.3 oz calvados

75 g/2.6 oz granulated sugar

Cake Batter:

100 g/3.5 oz almond flour

200 g/7.1 oz all-purpose flour

50 g/1.8 oz light brown sugar

10 g/0.35 oz (2 tsp) baking powder

Pinch of salt

6 eggs

100 g/3.5 oz almond oil

20 g/0.71 oz calvados

100 g/3.5 oz white chocolate chips

50 g/1.8 oz walnut pieces

Coating for the Pan:

Unsalted butter, at room temperature

Light brown sugar

Glaze:

100 g/3.5 oz heavy cream

75 g/2.6 oz dark chocolate chips

20 g/0.71 oz calvados

Apple #5
Apple Upside-Down Cake

For the brandied apples, combine the apple cubes and slices with calvados and sugar in a covered container. Allow the apple pieces to soak for a few hours or overnight.

Remove the macerated apple pieces from the calvados-sugar mixture using a strainer and reserve.

For the cake batter, in a mixer bowl, combine the almond flour, flour, sugar, baking powder, and salt. Attach the bowl to a stand mixer fitted with a paddle attachment. Mix well. Blend in the eggs, almond oil, and calvados. Mix again to combine. Finally, fold the reserved apple cubes, chocolate chips, and walnut pieces into the batter.

Generously butter a 23-cm/9-in round cake pan, and then evenly coat the bottom of the pan with light brown sugar. Arrange the reserved apple slices on top of the sugar. Pour the batter into the pan. Bake the cake at 188°C/370°F for about 40 minutes. Let the cake cool slightly before unmolding.

For the glaze, boil the cream in a saucepan, and then pour the hot cream over the dark chocolate chips in a mixing bowl. Stir the mixture until smooth. Add the calvados into the mixture. Glaze the cake with the icing. Allow the icing to set slightly before serving.

INGREDIENTS *(Yield: one 23-cm/9-in round cake)*

Brandied Apples:

1 Granny Smith apple, peeled and cut into cubes (around 175 g/6.2 oz)

75 g/2.6 oz calvados

38 g/1.3 oz granulated sugar

Cake Batter:

150 g/5.3 oz hazelnut flour

200 g/7.1 oz all-purpose flour

50 g/1.8 oz granulated sugar

10 g/0.35 oz (1 Tbsp) instant dry yeast

Pinch of salt

50 g/1.8 oz unsalted butter, at room temperature

100 g/3.5 oz cream cheese, at room temperature

2 eggs

200 g/7.1 oz whole milk

30 g/1.1 oz calvados

150 g/5.3 oz milk chocolate chips

100 g/3.5 oz walnut pieces

Glaze:

100 g/3.5 oz heavy cream

75 g/2.6 oz milk chocolate chips

20 g/0.71 oz calvados

50 g/1.8 oz whole roasted hazelnuts

Apple #6
Apple Bundt Cake

For the brandied apples, combine the apple cubes with calvados and sugar in a covered container. Allow the apple cubes to soak for a few hours or overnight.

Remove the macerated apple cubes from the calvados-sugar mixture using a strainer and reserve.

For the cake batter, in a mixer bowl, combine the hazelnut flour, flour, sugar, yeast, and salt. Attach the bowl to a stand mixer fitted with a paddle attachment. Mix well. Blend in the butter and cream cheese. Add the eggs, milk, and calvados. Mix again to combine. Finally, fold the reserved apple cubes, chocolate chips, and walnut pieces into the batter. Cover the bowl with plastic wrap, and allow the batter to rise overnight at room temperature.

On the following day, butter a 23-cm/9-in Bundt pan, and then pour the batter into the pan. Cover the pan with plastic wrap and allow the batter to rise at room temperature for 30 minutes. Bake the cake at 185°C/365°F for about 40 minutes. Unmold the cake when it is still warm.

For the glaze, boil the cream in a saucepan, and then pour the hot cream over the milk chocolate chips in a mixing bowl. Stir the mixture until smooth. Add the calvados and whole hazelnuts into the mixture. Glaze the cake with the icing. Allow the icing to set slightly before serving.

INGREDIENTS *(Yield: one 20-cm/8-in cake)*

Brandied Apples:

2 Granny Smith apples, peeled and cut into cubes (around 350 g/12.3 oz)

1 Granny Smith apple, peeled and cut into slices (around 175 g/6.2 oz)

225 g/7.9 oz calvados

113 g/4 oz granulated sugar

Cake Batter:

150 g/5.3 oz almond flour

250 g/8.8 oz all-purpose flour

100 g/3.5 oz granulated sugar

50 g/1.8 oz cocoa powder

15 g/0.53 oz (1 Tbsp) baking powder

5 g/0.18 oz (1 tsp) baking soda

Pinch of salt

100 g/3.5 oz unsalted butter, at room temperature

200 g/7.1 oz cream cheese, at room temperature

4 eggs

50 g/1.8 oz calvados

100 g/3.5 oz whole milk

Topping:

Walnut pieces

Granulated sugar

Apple #7
Dark Chocolate Apple and Walnut Cake

For the brandied apples, combine the apple cubes and slices with calvados and sugar in a covered container. Allow the apple pieces to soak for a few hours or overnight.

Remove the macerated apple pieces from the calvados-sugar mixture using a strainer and reserve.

For the cake batter, in a mixer bowl, combine the almond flour, flour, sugar, cocoa powder, baking powder, baking soda, and salt. Attach the bowl to a stand mixer fitted with a paddle attachment. Mix well. Blend in the softened butter and cream cheese. Add the eggs, calvados, and whole milk. Mix again to combine. Finally, fold the reserved apple cubes into the batter.

Generously butter a 20-cm/8-in tube pan, and then pour the batter into the pan. Arrange the reserved apple slices and walnut pieces on top of the batter. Sprinkle granulated sugar on top. Bake the cake at 185°C/365°F for about 40 minutes. Let cool slightly before unmolding.

INGREDIENTS *(Yield: one 20-cm/8-in loaf cake)*

Brandied Apples:

1 Granny Smith apple, peeled and cut into cubes (around 175 g/6.2 oz)

1 Granny Smith apple, peeled and cut into slices (around 175 g/6.2 oz)

150 g/5.3 oz calvados

75 g/2.6 oz granulated sugar

Cake Batter:

100 g/3.5 oz hazelnut flour

200 g/7.1 oz all-purpose flour

75 g/2.6 oz granulated sugar

30 g/1.1 oz cocoa powder

15 g/0.53 oz (1 Tbsp) baking powder

1.25 g/0.044 oz (¼ tsp) baking soda

Pinch of salt

100 g/3.5 oz unsalted butter, at room temperature

50 g/1.8 oz sour cream

100 g/3.5 oz apple puree

3 eggs

30 g/1.1 oz calvados

100 g/3.5 oz milk chocolate chips

70 g/2.5 oz macadamia nuts

Coating for the Pan:

Unsalted butter, at room temperature

Granulated sugar

Apple #8
Dark Chocolate Macadamia Apple Cake

For the brandied apples, combine the apple cubes and slices with calvados and sugar in a covered container. Allow the apple pieces to soak for a few hours or overnight.

Remove the macerated apple pieces from the calvados-sugar mixture using a strainer and reserve.

For the cake batter, in a mixer bowl, combine the hazelnut flour, flour, sugar, cocoa powder, baking powder, baking soda, and salt. Attach the bowl to a stand mixer fitted with a paddle attachment. Mix well. Blend in the softened butter and sour cream. Add the apple puree, eggs, and calvados. Mix again to combine. Finally fold the reserved apple cubes, chocolate chips, and macadamia nuts into the batter.

Butter a 20-cm/8-in loaf pan. Evenly coat the bottom of the pan with sugar. Arrange the reserved apple slices on top of the sugar. Pour the cake batter over the apple slices. Bake the cake at 185°C/365°F for about an hour. Let cool slightly before unmolding.

INGREDIENTS *(Yield: one 23-cm/9-in round cake)*

Brandied Pears:

1 Bartlett pear, peeled and cut into cubes (around 175 g/6.2 oz)

1 Bartlett pear, peeled and cut into slices (around 175 g/6.2 oz)

150 g/5.3 oz calvados

75 g/2.6 oz granulated sugar

Cake Batter:

100 g/3.5 oz almond flour

150 g/5.3 oz all-purpose flour

50 g/1.8 oz granulated sugar

10 g/0.35 oz (1 Tbsp) instant dry yeast

Pinch of salt

70 g/2.5 oz almond oil

50 g/1.8 oz sour cream

4 eggs

20 g/0.71 oz calvados

100 g/3.5 oz white chocolate chips

70 g/2.5 oz walnut pieces

Topping:

Unsalted butter, at room temperature

Granulated sugar

Apple #9
Chocolate Pear Round Cake

For the brandied pears, combine the pear cubes and slices with calvados and sugar in a covered container. Allow the pear pieces to soak for a few hours or overnight.

Remove the macerated pear pieces from the calvados-sugar mixture using a strainer and reserve.

For the cake batter, in a mixer bowl, combine the almond flour, flour, sugar, yeast, and salt. Attach the bowl to a stand mixer fitted with a paddle attachment. Mix well. Add the almond oil, sour cream, eggs, and calvados. Mix again to combine. Fold the reserved pear cubes, chocolate chips, and walnut pieces into the batter. Cover the bowl with plastic wrap. Allow the batter to rise at room temperature overnight.

On the following day, butter a 23-cm/9-in round cake pan. Evenly coat the bottom of the pan with sugar. Arrange the pear slices on top of the sugar. Pour the batter into the pan. Cover and let the batter rest at room temperature for about 40 minutes. Bake the cake at 191°C/375°F for about 40 minutes. Let cool slightly before unmolding.

INGREDIENTS *(Yield: two 20-cm/8-in cakes)*

Brandied Pears:

2 Bartlett pears, peeled and cut into cubes (around 350 g/12.3 oz)

150 g/5.3 oz calvados

75 g/2.6 oz granulated sugar

Cake Batter:

100 g/3.5 oz hazelnut flour

300 g/10.6 oz all-purpose flour

70 g/2.5 oz granulated sugar

50 g/1.8 oz cocoa powder

10 g/0.35 oz (1 Tbsp) instant dry yeast

Pinch of salt

50 g/1.8 oz unsalted butter, at room temperature

250 g/8.8 oz cream cheese, at room temperature

4 eggs

150 g/5.3 oz whole milk

50 g/1.8 oz calvados

70 g/2.5 oz macadamia nuts

100 g/3.5 oz white chocolate chips

Apple #10
Dark Chocolate Pear Cakes

For the brandied pears, combine the pear cubes with calvados and sugar in a covered container. Allow the pear cubes to soak for a few hours or overnight.

Remove the macerated pear cubes from the calvados-sugar mixture using a strainer and reserve.

For the cake batter, in a mixer bowl, combine the hazelnut flour, flour, sugar, cocoa powder, yeast, and salt. Attach the bowl to a stand mixer fitted with a paddle attachment. Mix well. Blend in the butter and cream cheese. Add the eggs, milk, and calvados. Mix again to combine. Finally, fold the reserved pear cubes, macadamia nuts, and chocolate chips into the batter. Cover the bowl with plastic wrap. Allow the batter to rise at room temperature overnight.

On the following day, butter two 20-cm/8-in brioche molds, and then pour the batter into the molds. Cover and let the batter rest at room temperature for about 40 minutes. Bake the cakes at 185°C/365°F for 35 minutes. Let cool slightly before unmolding.

INGREDIENTS *(Yield: one 20-cm/8-in cake)*

Brandied Pears:

2 Bartlett pears, peeled and cut into cubes (around 350 g/12.3 oz)

1 Bartlett pear, peeled and cut into slices (around 175 g/6.2 oz)

225 g/7.9 oz calvados

113 g/4 oz granulated sugar

Cake Batter:

100 g/3.5 oz hazelnut flour

300 g/10.6 oz all-purpose flour

100 g/3.5 oz granulated sugar

15 g/0.53 oz (1 Tbsp) baking powder

2.5 g/0.088 oz (½ tsp) baking soda

Pinch of salt

150 g/5.3 oz unsalted butter, at room temperature

100 g/3.5 oz cream cheese, at room temperature

3 eggs

50 g/1.8 oz calvados

200 g/7.1 oz whole milk

150 g/5.3 oz milk chocolate chips

70 g/2.5 oz walnut pieces

Topping:

Walnut pieces

60 g/2.1 oz softened cream cheese

1 egg yolk

Granulated sugar

Apple #11
Milk Chocolate Hazelnut Pear Cake

For the brandied pears, combine the pear cubes and slices with calvados and sugar in a covered container. Allow the pear pieces to soak for a few hours or overnight.

Remove the macerated pear pieces from the calvados-sugar mixture using a strainer and reserve.

For the cake batter, in a mixer bowl, combine the hazelnut flour, flour, sugar, baking powder, baking soda, and salt. Attach the bowl to a stand mixer fitted with a paddle attachment. Mix well. Blend in the butter and cream cheese. Add the eggs, calvados, and milk. Mix again to combine. Finally, fold the reserved pear cubes, chocolate chips, and walnut pieces into the batter.

Butter a 20-cm/8-in tube pan, and then pour the batter into the pan. Place the reserved pear slices and walnuts on top. Mix the cream cheese and egg yolk. Add the mixture over the pears. Sprinkle sugar on top. Bake the cake at 185°C/365°F for about 45 minutes. Let cool slightly before unmolding.

INGREDIENTS *(Yield: three 20-cm/8-in loaf cakes)*

Brandied Apples:

2 Granny Smith apples, peeled and cut into small cubes (around 350 g/12.3 oz)

150 g/5.3 oz calvados

75 g/2.6 oz granulated sugar

Cake Batter:

150 g/5.3 oz almond flour

300 g/10.6 oz all-purpose flour

120 g/4.2 oz granulated sugar

22.5 g/0.8 oz (1½ Tbsp) baking powder

Pinch of salt

300 g/10.6 oz cream cheese, at room temperature

4 eggs

15 g/0.53 oz (1 Tbsp) vanilla extract

150 g/5.3 oz heavy cream

100 g/3.5 oz whole milk (A)

40 g/1.4 oz calvados

20 g/0.7 oz cocoa powder

20 g/0.7 oz whole milk (B)

100 g/3.5 oz walnut pieces

100 g/3.5 oz dried cranberries

Apple #12
Apple Marble Cakes

For the brandied apples, combine the apple cubes with calvados and sugar in a covered container. Allow the apple cubes to soak for a few hours or overnight.

Remove the macerated apple cubes from the calvados-sugar mixture using a strainer and reserve.

For the cake batter, in a mixer bowl, combine the almond flour, flour, sugar, baking powder, and salt. Attach the bowl to a stand mixer fitted with a paddle attachment. Add the cream cheese, eggs, vanilla extract, cream, milk (A), and calvados. Mix all the ingredients into a batter.

For the chocolate batter, pour about 200 g/7.1 oz of the cake batter into a second mixing bowl. Add the cocoa powder and milk (B). Mix well.

Fold the reserved apple cubes, walnuts, and dried cranberries into the first batch of batter.

Butter three 20-cm x 10-cm/8-in x 4-in narrow loaf pans; equally divide the first batch of batter among the pans. Add the chocolate batter on top. Use a fork to stir the batter and therefore producing the marbling effect. Bake the loaves at 185°C/365°F for about 35 minutes. Let cool slightly before unmolding.

INGREDIENTS *(Yield: one 20-cm/8-in loaf cake)*

Brandied Apples:

1 Granny Smith apple, peeled and cut into small cubes (around 175 g/6.2 oz)

75 g/2.6 oz calvados

38 g/1.3 oz granulated sugar

Cake Dough:

275 g/9.7 oz all-purpose floor

10 g/0.35 oz (1 Tbsp) instant dry yeast

30 g/1.1 oz granulated sugar

Pinch of salt

100 g/3.5 oz whole milk

1 egg

70 g/2.5 oz unsalted butter, at room temperature

Topping:

30 g/1.1 oz almond paste

30 g/1.1 oz heavy cream

1 egg

20 g/0.71 oz calvados

50 g/1.8 oz dark chocolate chips

Apple #13
Apple Coffee Cake

For the brandied apples, combine the apple cubes with calvados and sugar in a covered container. Allow the apple cubes to soak for a few hours or overnight.

For the cake dough, in a mixer bowl, combine the flour, yeast, sugar, salt, milk, egg, and butter. Attach the bowl to a stand mixer fitted with a dough hook attachment. Knead the dough for about 10 minutes. Cover the bowl with plastic wrap and let the dough rest for 30 minutes at room temperature. After that, allow the dough to rise in the refrigerator overnight.

On the following day, remove the macerated apple cubes from the calvados-sugar mixture using a strainer and reserve.

Remove the dough from the refrigerator. Divide the dough into 10 pieces and shape each piece into a ball. Butter a 20-cm/8-in tube pan. Arrange the dough balls in the pan. Cover the pan and allow the dough to rise at room temperature for about two hours or until doubled in volume.

Meanwhile, mix the almond paste, cream, egg, and calvados into a paste and reserve. Before baking, sprinkle the reserved apple cubes and chocolate chips on top of the dough, and then add the reserved almond-calvados paste on top of the dough. Bake the cake at 185°C/365°F for about 40 minutes. Let cool slightly before unmolding.

www.ingramcontent.com/pod-product-compliance
Lightning Source LLC
Chambersburg PA
CBHW061731070526
44583CB00024B/3096